Dedicated

to the memory of

Dorothy Jean Caldwell

who loved Kansas City

and its people.

US SPRINT presents

Focus Kansas City

A 24-Hour Heartland Portrait

David S. Hudson — *Editor*

Rich Clarkson — *Editor of Photography*

Rick Cusick — *Designer*

Robert Eisele — *Editorial Associate*

Jody Buie — *Editorial Associate*

HARROW BOOKS
Prairie Village, Kansas

Focus Kansas City: A 24-Hour Heartland Portrait
First Printing : September, 1989

©1989 Harrow Books
a division of Hudson & Associates, Inc.
Prairie Village, Kansas

ISBN Number: 0-91-6455-07-6
Library of Congress Catalog Card Number: 89-085897

Printed in the United States of America

Corporate Sponsors

US Sprint

AAA Auto Club
Andy Klein Pontiac-GMC
Ashcraft, Inc.
Ask Mr. Foster
Blue Cross and Blue Shield of Kansas City
B. C. Christopher Securities Company
Commerce Bank
Ernst & Whinney
Farmland Industries, Inc.
Fleming Companies, Inc.
Hallmark Cards, Inc.
Howard Needles Tammen & Bergendoff
Hudson & Associates, Inc.
Johnson County Community College
Kansas City Board of Trade
KLSI
Lathrop Koontz & Norquist
Long Motor Corporation
McGrew Color Graphics
Morrison, Hecker, Curtis, Kuder & Parrish
J. D. Nelson Building Company
North Kansas City Hospital
J. D. Reece Realtors
Catherine Rickbone
Rockhurst College
Shalom Geriatric Center
Stinson, Mag & Fizzell
University of Missouri-Kansas City School of Dentistry
Western Auto
Wetterau Incorporated

Friends of Focus Kansas City

Alpha-Omega Typesetting
B'Gosh & B'Golly
Koch Supplies, Inc.
MCD Construction
Olde Theatre Architectural Salvage Company
Preferred Elegant Garden Supplies

 **US Sprint** ®

In three short years, US Sprint has emerged as one of the nation's top three long-distance companies. The rise of this Kansas City-based company was the combined result of a unique opportunity and a visionary idea.

Soon after the telephone industry was deregulated in 1984, a Kansas City company called United Telecommunications decided to make a bold bid for a strong position in the burgeoning long-distance market. The plan: to build from scratch a 23,000-mile fiber optic network to service the entire continental United States. Only five years later this state of the art system is complete, providing a new standard of clear "pin-drop quality" sound. The expanding company provides long-distance voice and data communications services domestically and around the world.

US Sprint has already chalked up an impressive string of marketing victories. Today its customer base includes more than 90 percent of the Fortune 500 companies, millions of residential customers, and a 40 percent share of the federal government's multi-billion dollar telephone services contract.

In combination with its parent and majority owner United Telecommunications, US Sprint makes a major contribution to the Kansas City area economy. The companies together employ over 6,000 Kansas Citians. Salaries and benefits paid in the metropolitan area top $200 million. And local and state income taxes pouring into Missouri and Kansas exceed $10 million annually. US Sprint occupies 23 buildings in the area, including Missouri's tallest office building, One Kansas City Place.

Nationally, US Sprint and United Telecom employ over 37,000 people, who work for a family of related companies that also includes United Telephone local operating companies providing service to 3,000 communities in 17 states; North Supply (a telephone equipment distributor), and Sprint Services, a provider of operator and "900" information services.

Rooted in the heartland of America, US Sprint and United Telecom posted 1988 revenues exceeding $6 billion and assets of more than $9 billion. This placed United Telecom among America's top 200 companies, and Kansas City as a major center for one of the nation's leading growth industries.

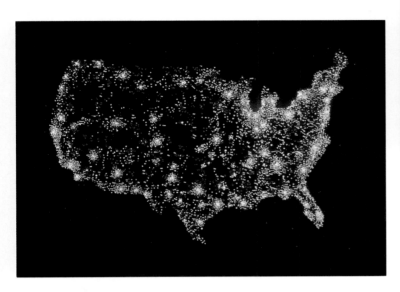

Fiber-optic technology uses laser light pulses through hair-thin strands of glass to transmit voice, data and video signals. US Sprint is extending its 23,000 mile domestic fiber-optic network across the oceans to provide "pin-drop quality" sound around the world.

Kansas City . . . the heart of America and the heartbeat of US Sprint's all-digital, all fiber-optic network. The National Operations Control Center monitors traffic on the network 24 hours a day, seven days a week.

VEDROS & ASSOCIATES

Chairman of the board of United Tele-communications, Inc., is Paul H. Henson (left), who led the company's innovation of a nationwide fiber optic network. With him is William T. Esrey, president and chief executive officer of the company, who believes Kansas City is destined to become a major telecommunications hub.

Located at 8140 Ward Parkway is the corporate headquarters for US Sprint, the nation's fastest-growing provider of long-distance service.

9

Introduction

As a four-year-old in Wichita just before World War II, I was as mystified as a Pacific island aborigine by the pictures of myself that appeared hours or days after my father pointed a bulky black box at me and tripped a lever. There I was, usually with my younger sister, just as I had stood in the garden, but now fixed and immobile in a black-and-white image on paper.

I was told that this was "taking a picture," but it wasn't until my father took me into his makeshift darkroom (the transformed bathroom of our rented house) and allowed me to watch the developing and printing procedures, that I began to sense intuitively certain connections between the process and the result.

My first camera, a sleek little Brownie Hawkeye, was acquired when I was 13 years old. Already fascinated by the photographs I saw in the newspaper, I convinced the manager of the visiting Clyde Beatty Circus to allow me to go "backstage" and photograph the performers prior to a performance. The photos turned out surprisingly well, especially the one of the spangled lady who posed while perched on an elephant's trunk.

My first professional encounter with a camera came in 1957 when, as a reporter for the *Topeka State Journal*, I was occasionally required to take one of the company's Speed Graphics and shoot a picture for a reporting assignment.

These cumbersome behemoths were not, to understate the case, "user friendly." It was about this time that the management hired an inventive young photographer named Rich Clarkson. He moved the newspaper out of the dark ages of "news pictures" into a new era of photojournalism made possible by the widening use of the 35mm camera.

Clarkson became a much-admired standard-setter in his profession nationally. He was director of photography for the highly successful *A Day in the Life of America*, the inspiration for this volume, for which he generously consented to be photo editor.

It was *A Day in the Life of America* that set me to thinking that a similar collection of photographs about people in the Kansas City metropolitan region could (A) provide a photodocumentary profile of our community life; and (B) offer a collection of visually arresting pictures enjoyable as first-rate photographic art.

A few other communities have embarked on similar projects, usually through non-profit photo clubs. Just such a project, Miami's *Picture South Florida*, served as a model for the Kansas City project. Dennie Cody, a key figure in the Miami endeavor, was Harrow Books' guest at an orientation session to brief our photographers about what to expect and how to deal with the vagaries of a 24-hour shooting schedule.

To aid the funding of this expensive project, Harrow enlisted the financial support of area business and industry. Some three dozen business leaders became

Focus Kansas City *editor David Hudson holds a sheet of transparencies to be reviewed by screening participants (standing, from left) Larry Nicholson and Steve Wilson. Seated at right is committee assistant David Wirtz. (Photograph by Bob Barrett)*

page sponsors. Their corporate profiles will be found starting on page 194.

But the "anchor" sponsor for the book became US Sprint, the long distance division of United Telecommunications, Inc., which has its headquarters in Fairway, Kan. US Sprint's generous grant funded a major portion of the book's cost as well as a handsome traveling exhibition of more than three dozen photographs from the book. This exhibition will be on display in various public facilities in the Kansas City area throughout most of 1990.

Even as funding for the book was sought, area photographic organizations were contacted and their members invited to participate. None of these groups was directly involved in the conduct of the project, but many of their members were among the 117 photographers who signed on for the midnight-to-midnight shoot on Wednesday, October 5, 1988.

Harrow Books provided each photographer with three or four prearranged assignments, but each participant was encouraged to photograph "targets of opportunity" throughout the day. To accomplish this Harrow gave the photographers more than 1,500 rolls of Fujicolor film — coded to assure that all film returned was shot in the specified 24-hour time frame.

What happened on October 5, 1988, was — quite simply — the largest single-day photojournalism project ever undertaken in Kansas City's five-county metropolitan area. Hundreds of Kansas Citians were photographed as they went

Rich Clarkson, editor of photography for Focus Kansas City, *evaluated more than 1,200 transparencies before selecting some 230 candidates for use in the book. Designer Rick Cusick utilized 210 in the final page configurations. (Photograph by Bob Barrett)*

about their work and play that day. The aim was not to create a "pretty" picture book of Kansas City's physical beauty, but a document that made an arresting, truthful statement about the way our Heartland residents conduct their lives on a single, randomly selected day.

Even with the impressive number of picture-takers at work, such an effort could not claim to be totally comprehensive. Instead, it is a selective mosaic of images that are representative of the range of community activity taking place that day — from education, business and the arts, to government, agriculture and leisure. In all, over 36,000 images were produced on 35mm color transparencies, these to be expertly processed by Custom Color laboratories.

Less than one percent of the pictures taken — slightly more than 200 — would be used in the book. The selection of these was a three-tiered process that began with myself, as editor, doing a cursory (three ten-hour days!) run-through of all 36,000 transparencies. No subtle esthetics were involved at this stage, only a weeding out of images that were technically deficient — out of focus, incorrectly lighted, improperly framed, etc. This quickly reduced the usable candidates to 5,000. In a subsequent two-day viewing session, I was joined by Larry Nicholson of Nicholson Productions, and Steve Wilson, a senior photographer with Hallmark Cards, in selecting about 1,100 images that, technically and esthetically, were "book quality." A few weeks later, Rich Clarkson came from his Denver home to make the final editorial cut — these selections forming the reservoir of images to be used.

With a few exceptions, virtually all of Clarkson's selections made it into the book. Design continuity, thematic balance, subject matter redundancy, and technical considerations influenced the ultimate selection and placement of pictures by book designer Rick Cusick. He quickly saw the "family album" quality of the work to be included, and so there is no formal arrangement of material by subject, chronology or geographic location. Nevertheless, Cusick's designer sensibilities discovered certain patterns and connections that influenced placement and arrangement in quite remarkable juxtapositions.

Working from photographers' notes and often talking directly with the subjects in the pictures, editorial associates Robert Eisele and Jody Buie further enriched the visual experience with supportive information. Both these valued assistants played key roles in virtually every aspect of the project from first to last.

But, of course, this book would not have been created without the talents of the participating photographers. Functioning independently within the project's broad parameters, they became photo historians through whose eyes we and our heirs will be able to experience and evaluate the essence and the specifics of a typical day in our community.

During the day of the shoot and for weeks thereafter reports filtered back about the pleasures the photographers and their subjects had taken in this documentary exercise. Photographer Mike Mihalevich, a seasoned professional, captured the day's "high" and "low" — in relation to the earth's surface. At dawn he was in a plane shooting the sun's first rays as they glanced off skyscrapers. Later in the day, armed with an underwater camera, he photographed students in a scuba diving class.

Several photographers spoke of the spirit of cooperation that accompanied their efforts throughout the 24-hour shooting period. When John Perryman's pickup truck got stuck in the mud at Stephenson's Apple Orchard, owner Ron Stephenson was recruited to pull him out. Chris Cannella, discovering that her camera's batteries had suddenly gone dead, received a spare set from another (unidentified) photographer in the *Focus* project. Vietnamese refugees assembling silk clothing at a River Market studio invited photographer John Clark to join them for lunch after he took their picture.

Vernon Leat, en route to an assignment, happened by accident on a group of demonstrators in front of the Environmental Protection Agency office in Kansas City, Kan. Just as unexpected was Don Wolf's discovery of a dramatic fire on Interstate 635 near State Avenue in Kansas City, Kan. On his way back to his studio, he reloaded his empty camera fast enough to capture a truck engulfed in flames. The violence of that moment was of a different kind than that encountered by Wolf on the trading floor of the Kansas City Board of Trade earlier in the day. "They (the traders) went from doing absolutely nothing to total frenzy in a matter of seconds," said Wolf. "The procedure seems to combine sophisticated functions with fairly primitive methods."

When Bob Sabin went to photograph the "Scout" statue in Penn Valley Park, he encountered a couple, romantically engaged in the secluded spot. They looked up only momentarily as Sabin went about his business.

Wally Emerson got to do what few other men are permitted: view the male strip show at Apple Jack's nightclub in Merriam. "The women went wild," he reported, "and the dancers made me feel even skinnier than I am." But Debbie Douglass Sauer kept her cool when the surgeon she was photographing at K.U. Medical Center invited her into the operating room during surgery. Outfitted in a surgical scrub suit, Debbie photographed the procedure and later said that "not fainting was my biggest thrill of the day."

Harrow Books was especially pleased that a disabled photographer, wheelchair-bound Kevin Robinson, handled a number of assignments. The high point of his day was getting permission from folk singer Arlo Guthrie's management to photograph the performer on stage at the Uptown Theater. "The *Focus* project was way beyond anything I had tried before," Kevin said. "It was a physical challenge, but pure fun and excitement, too."

Laura Maxwell Shultz was recuperating from surgery on shoot day, but she still managed to complete several assignments with the help of her sons, David and Doug. Randy Braun shared a parents' joy within the first few minutes following their son's birth at Menorah Medical Center, but was saddened when he photographed a victim of Lou Gehrig's disease later that day. The man, James T. (Pete) Oliver, died on New Year's Day, 1989.

Life and death, achievement and failure, triumph and tragedy, joy and despair — these are reflected in many of the photos to be found in the pages that follow. But they are the threads that weave their way in and out of life's fabric every day, and our photographers have caught them in affecting ways. The images are alternately beautiful, funny, sentimental, touching, irritating and inspiring.

But whatever they are, they are us — captured on one arbitrary day late in the 20th Century and preserved in a family album we call *Focus Kansas City*.

David S. Hudson, Editor

Three-year-old Chantal Kester gets a close-up view of the Northland Fountain at North Oak Trafficway and Vivion Road in Gladstone, Mo. Designed by the Hydrel Company of Sun Valley, Calif., this recent addition to the "City of Fountains" is modeled after a similar one in Stuttgart, Germany. Featuring an 80-foot diameter circular reflecting pool and a central geyser that propels water to a height of 35 feet, the fountain is designed for year-round operation. The Northland Fountain was dedicated in June, 1983.

Photographer:
Alan Kester

If he isn't mowing the lawn for one of his 15 widow friends, John Schrantz, 75, of Kansas City, Mo., divines astrology sayings to write on the weatherproof black board in his front yard. Schrantz, retired from 47 years work at St. Mary's Hospital and life-long resident of Kansas City, became involved in astrology during World War II in Germany. His displayed messages come from astrology books, or from thoughts he has from the gossip he hears, or from the mood in which he awakes. He changes the sayings of the board every other day, or more often if one is found to be offensive and he is asked to change it sooner.

Photographer:
Bob Travaglione

Like father, like son. As cub master of pack no. 27, Frank James, Sr. of Kansas City, Mo., has just helped his nine-year-old son, Frank, Jr. memorize the preamble to the Constitution, one of the requirements to move up in the Webelo rank of Cub Scouts. Frank Sr., who has spent 38 of his 46 years in scouting, believes it provides the structure to develop young men into successful, productive citizens, which is his dream for his son, a fourth-year cub scout and fourth grader at St. Peters Catholic School in Kansas City, Mo. Frank Sr. is a 4-H youth specialist at the Kansas City extension office of the University of Missouri Columbia.

Photographer:
Rudy Yanez

Man's best friend and security manager, Cholly's Red Choice (aka "Red"), guards Nova Products for his master, Boyce E. Carson. Carson, 32, is president of the pesticide manufacturing company founded by his grandfather. Red, a Doberman Pinscher, is named after his great-great-great grandfather, Cholly's Choice, which Carson owned as a teenager.

Photographer:
Julie Robertson

Trainer Dot Wartenberg puts pupils at the Canine College in Kansas City, Kan., through their paces. Dot's system of obedience training is based on the three P's: patience, persistence and praise. In the eight-week session, dogs learn to respond to about 35 commands. Canine College alumni can return anytime for a refresher course.

Photographer:
Bob Barrett

Joe McKechnie enjoys the twilight solitude of Shawnee Mission Park to get in some serious fishing. McKechnie's dog, Taro, has his own agenda as he explores the marina dock.

Photographer:
David Brandt

Sponsor: McGREW COLOR GRAPHICS

During a commercial break on the 5 p.m. newscast, weatherman Dan Henry (left) "takes five," while anchor Bob Thill awaits a cue. Henry, a former Topeka school teacher, joined WDAF-TV in 1959. Thill worked for a St. Joseph TV station before joining WDAF as a general assignment reporter in 1980. On October 5, Henry was predicting "sweater weather" as the season's first cold front moved through the area.

Among the top local stories: A Kansas City, Kan., man kept police at bay for two hours while holding his wife and child hostage, and a pair of Kansas City teenagers went on a $30,000 shopping spree at Bannister Mall after allegedly stealing a quarter million dollars in drug money. Since no theft was reported, no charges were filed.

Photographer:
Mark McCabe

Michael Goldman — the man and the caricature — stand outside Plumbers Friend at 83rd and Wornall. Having grown up in the plumbing supply business, Goldman founded his own company in 1983. Doug Norton, one of his three employees, is the talented caricaturist.

Photographer:
Bob Travaglione

John Bichelmeyer founded Bichelmeyer's Meats in the Armourdale District of Kansas City, Kan., in 1946. Though the flood of 1951 destroyed his business, Bichelmeyer rebuilt his shop. Today, it's one of the few remaining family-owned butcher shops in the city. Bichelmeyer runs the slaughterhouse that processes about 2,000 head of cattle and hogs a year. His three sons run the retail meat market across the street.

Photographer:
Kevin Robinson

Take-out barbecue is wrapped by Terry Stewart, assistant manager of Arthur Bryant's Barbecue at 18th and Brooklyn. Launched by brothers Arthur and Charlie Bryant, this 50-year-old establishment is a mecca for barbecue lovers. Once the food of the poor and unemployed, barbecue has attained almost gourmet status in present-day Kansas City. More than 60 barbecue restaurants are found in the metro area.

Photographer:
LeRoy Scott

Michael Warren, a baker at Andre's Confiserie Suisse at 5018 Main in Kansas City, takes a batch of apple turnovers out of the oven near the beginning of his 4 a.m. to 2 p.m. shift. Warren supervises all the baking for the tea room and bakery, turning out dozens of croissants, coffee cakes, quiche and French pastries daily for the past 15 years. ''We make everything from scratch, so you're really creating something,'' Warren says.

Photographer:
Victor Almo

Some familiar Kansas City names dot the tombstones at St. Mary's Cemetery at 2201 Cleveland. Descendants of the French fur-trapping Chouteaus are buried here, as are some members of the Troost family. Founded in 1874 by Father Bernard Donnelly, the 43-acre cemetery is the city's third oldest.

Photographer:
John Clark

A streetside vendor finds few takers for his furry menagerie on this quiet midweek afernoon. The ''stuffed animals to go'' concession is set up in the parking lot of an abandoned service station near 63rd Street and the Paseo.

Photographer:
Ben Mercer

Members of the Northeast High School varsity cross country team participate in a daily workout regimen, which includes a run of four to 10 miles. Seen here running along Cliff Drive near the Kansas City Museum, Coach Ray Wade's team was the 1988 Interscholastic League Champion.

To prepare for the five-kilometer competition, the 15-to-18-year-olds train with long-distance runs, weight training, swimming and bicycling.

Photographer:
Vernon Leat

A construction boom dating to the mid-1980s resulted in more than $800 million in new construction and rehabilitation of existing buildings in Kansas City. That was good news to people like Lloyd Graybill (hard hat) and Tim Carroll (sunglasses), employees of the Lawson Steel Co. On October 5, Graybill and Carroll took time out from assembling a steel frame for a skylight in the One Kansas City Place for a photo.

Photographer:
Bob Barrett

Cartoonist Charles Barsotti's work appears regularly in the *New Yorker* and daily in *USA Today*. This 55-year-old Texas native has lived in Kansas City since 1963, when he came to work at Hallmark Cards as an artist/writer.

Photographer:
William Kirk

Sponsor: HUDSON & ASSOCIATES, INC.

Kansas Citians are taking to the road on their bicycles in increasing numbers, and Midwest Cyclery shop owner Gus Baandrus is equipped to deal with the trend. Baandrus, who immigrated to the United States from Holland in 1960, opened his first bicycle shop in Kansas City in 1974. He now owns four stores, including this one on Johnson Drive in Mission, Kan.

Photographer:
Randy Braun

J.D. Nelson began building homes 25 years ago, and now heads his own Platte County construction company. Nelson inspects a home under construction in the Riss Lake development near Parkville, Mo. In October, Nelson had 30 homes in various stages of development in Platte and western Clay counties.

Photographer:
John Perryman

"The First Circle: Light Sculpture by Dale Eldred" was the current exhibit in October at Kansas City's Contemporary Art Center. "Dale works in light and the passage of time," explains photographer Ben Weddle, who employed a double exposure to help illustrate the effect of Eldred's exhibit. The work consists of 15-20 cones sprayed with phosphorescent paint and lighted by photographic strobes positioned above them. The strobes flashed every 15 seconds, leaving a lingering visual image. Eldred, chairman of the sculpture department at the Kansas City Art Institute, works with large-scale light sculptures incorporating reflective, diffractive and phosphorescent materials. His sculptures have been commissioned by such institutions as the Nelson-Atkins Museum of Art in Kansas City and the Helsinki City Art Museum in Finland.

Photographer:
Ben Weddle

Beginning at age three, students of the Suzuki method of developing music ability learn by observation and imitation. The nonprofit Music/Arts Institute in Independence instructs students in the Suzuki method, and parents assist by attending all lessons and supervising home practice. The Institute also conducts classes in classical ballet, creative movement and the visual arts for children ages 3-12.

Photographer:
Ron Berg

Professor Robert Batty rehearses graduate student Anne Berquist at the University of Missouri-Kansas City Conservatory of Music. Berquist, a native of France, began studying the cello at the age of eight, joining her older brothers on the piano and violin to form a family trio.

Photographer:
Steve Dawson

Sponsor: MORRISON, HECKER, CURTIS, KUDER & PARRISH

A French horn player since he was nine, Steve Rinehart, 17, holds the first chair position in the Lee's Summit Symphonic Band. Shown here weighted down with 30 medals for achievements in mathematics, music and science, this high school senior plans to attend the Massachusetts Institute of Technology and become a consulting engineer or experimental scientist. The horn he is carrying is a mellophone.

Photographer:
Bill Van Pelt

"Businessman by day, body-builder by night." That's how 29-year-old Chris Talarico describes his life. Talarico, a certified financial planner, has been training with 35-year-old registered nurse Roxian Jarboe for nearly six years. The two spend about two hours a day, six days a week at Moffet's Gym in Lenexa working out with weights to improve their body symmetry and muscle tone. Talarico has placed in the Heart of the Midwest and Mr. Kansas competitions, while Jarboe was a finalist in the USA Bodybuilding Championships in 1984. "It's kind of addictive," admits Jarboe, "although the dieting gets to be less fun as you get older."

Photographer:
Randy Braun

This skeleton by any other name is a coat rack. Located in an anesthesiologist's office at Shawnee Mission Medical Center, these plastic bones are used to teach patients about anatomy. At other times the skeleton holds humorous or health related messages for doctors between its teeth. The 383-bed hospital is one of the largest health care providers in Johnson County, Kan., and specializes in surgery.

Photographer:
Larry Tretbar

At Apple Jack's nightclub in Merriam, Kan., Brett Fuller (a.k.a. "Maverick" and "Ninja"), part of the "Body Heat" company of male dancers, struts his stuff before an enthusiastic crowd. Fuller, a native of Austin, Tex., began his dancing career two years ago at the urging of some friends who were in the business. He earns what he calls "a steady income" performing full-time, five nights a week at clubs within a 200-mile radius of Kansas City. Fuller begins his routines dressed in a flight suit or Ninja warrior's outfit, then strips down as a crowd of female admirers urges him on.

Photographer:
Wally Emerson

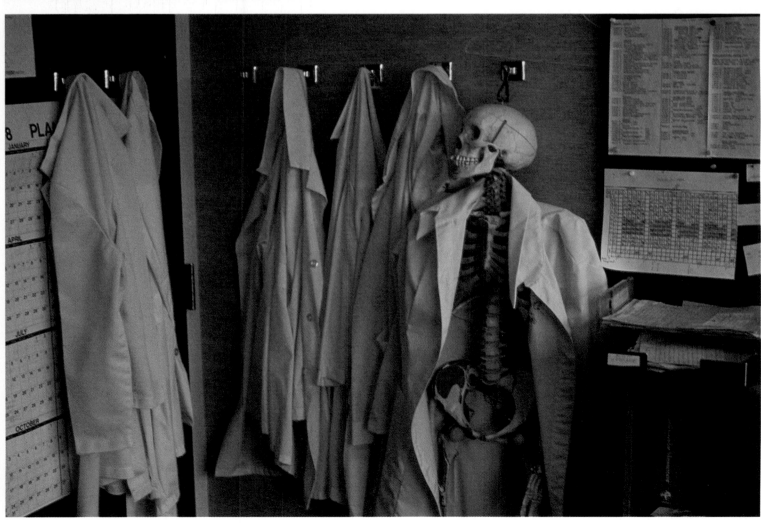

Wilbur Niewald, honorary senior professor of painting at the Kansas City Art Institute, captured the 12th street viaduct on canvas from a lookout point on Quality Hill in Kansas City, Mo. Having taken two months to complete, the painting was to be shown at an exhibition with a collection of Niewald's paintings at Dorry Gates Gallery in Kansas City. A life-long Kansas City resident and graduate of Southeast High School and the Kansas City Art Institute, he has taught at the Institute for 40 years and was recipient of the Distinguished Teaching of Art Award by the College Art Association of America in 1988.

Photographer:
John Vawter

Eight-year-old Charlie Sauer, a third grader at Valley Park Elementary in Overland Park, is a self-described Kansas City Royals fanatic who dreams of a career in the major leagues. Charlie's mom, photographer Debbie Sauer, shot this portrait of her son as he relaxed after school.

Photographer:
Debbie Douglass Sauer

Natasha can hardly believe her eyes. Alene Wesner of south Kansas City is signing the adoption papers to take her home. It was the first adoption Wesner had made from Wayside Waifs Humane Society, a non-profit charitable organization. More than 10,000 animals went through the animal shelter in 1988, most of which were placed in homes, thanks, in part, to the media. Radio station Q104 has a daily "pet of the day" feature to inform listeners of animals needing a home.

Photographer:
Don Yaworski

Arithmetic is OK, but six-year-old Rory Kane's favorite subject is reading. Rory is a straight-A first-grader at St. Therese School in Parkville.

Photographer:
Dave Swoboda

At Hawthorne Elementary School in Kansas City, Kan., five-year-old Nikeya Arnold was proud to have been selected room monitor for the day. Her official duties included checking attendance on a computerized roll sheet.

Photographer:
Chris Cannella

Broadway veteran and Kansas City native Myldred Lyons instructs a chorus line of hopeful dance enthusiasts. A dancer since the age of eight, Lyons toured all over the country and appeared on Broadway in 1928 with Irene Dunne in "Luckee Girl." She opened her own dance studio in 1939, instructing students of all ages on the art of dance. Before settling into her suburban Corinth Square studio, Lyons conducted classes in the dome of the Empire Theater building.

Photographer:
Ron Berg

The last trolley streetcar ran in Kansas City on June 23, 1957. In a scaled-down version, however, they still operate in the basement of 70-year-old Robert Moseley of Merriam, Kan. Moseley, a Kansas City streetcar operator from 1943 to 1950 and a volunteer fire fighter for the past 46 years, has built more than 400 feet of train track and trolley line and nearly 180 railroad and trolley cars. Built from scratch, each is a scale replica of the trolleys that were used in Kansas City — complete with pipecleaner passengers and conductors. Moseley, retired from Mobay Chemical Corp., takes his models to schools, discusses transportation with children and shows them how to make pipe cleaner figures.

Photographer:
LeRoy Scott
52

An aerial view reveals the ribbons of highway that make up part of Kansas City's transportation network. This view looking southwest from North Kansas City shows sections of Bedford Avenue on the left and Missouri Highway 210 on the right. Also visible are the Ralston Purina grain elevators at the top right.

Photographer:
Dave Bahm

Jim Covington has been working on the railroad for 33 years. Since 1987, he has coordinated traffic at the terminal tower of the Santa Fe Railway Co., which maintains the biggest yard in Kansas City. An average of 5,000 cars move through the Santa Fe facility each day.

Photographer:
Dave Swoboda

"It's big!" is the comment 16-year-old Cindy Schmidt, a junior at Ruskin High School, hears most often about her hairstyle. Encouraged by her boyfriend who plays in a rock band and has a similar hairstyle, she is not bothered by the comments of others. Rock concerts, meeting people, and photography are the activities Cindy enjoys most.

Photographer:
Chris Williams

Fifteen-year-old James Montgomery returns from an afternoon of mowing lawns near his home in Merriam, Kan. James said he was saving his money to buy a motorcycle.

Photographer:
Julie Denesha

Diligence is first nature to 14-year-old Richard Pinkney of Kansas City, Mo., an aspirant to the rank of Eagle Scout, which he hoped to have within three months with troop 608. He also serves as a den leader for the Webelos pack 27, where for the past three years he has helped younger boys earn their achievement awards. Pinkney is also a volunteer patient escort at Baptist Memorial Hospital. As an escort, he transports wheelchair patients as they are admitted, released and on their way to surgery. A freshman at Van Horn High School in Kansas City, Mo., Pinkney enjoys collecting baseball cards and hopes to become a military policeman.

Photographer:
Rudy Yanez

◁ Leo Hirner, assistant curator at the Kansas City Museum Planetarium, likes to introduce children to the wonders of the night sky. Hirner conducts programs on the stars and planets for schoolchildren during the week and in public programs on weekends. The planetarium is housed in what was once the conservatory of the northeast Kansas City mansion built by lumber baron R.A. Long.

Photographer:
Mark McCabe

Eighty-three-year-old Mildred Day suffers from a blood disorder in her leg, but she's determined to maintain her independence at her Riverside home. Day is visited three times a week by nurse Rebecca Wells of Kendallwood Home Health, an agency providing home care for patients still capable of looking after themselves. Day enjoys reading and watching TV, especially the Geraldo Rivera talk show.

Photographer:
Robert Sabin

Theater League president Mark Edelman (right) shares plans for an $850,000 renovation of the Midland Theater with J. Roland Wilson, executive director of the Folly Theater (left) and Scott Smalley, a painting contractor. Designed by architect Thomas Lamb (the most prolific of the movie palace designers), the Midland opened amid much fanfare in October, 1927. It was said to be movie magnate Marcus Loew's favorite theater. The screen went dark in 1982, and now the 2,854-seat Midland Center for the Performing Arts is home to concerts, dance events and touring productions of Broadway plays and musicals.

Photographer:
Bob Barrett

Although the fruit and vegetable stand that William Masucci (right) operates in the City Market has been in his family since 1895, none of his three children is interested in taking over the business. Nicknamed ''Boots'' by market regulars because of his oversize footwear, he began working at his grandfather's stand when he was nine years old. Today he tends the stand alone through the week, but his wife, Loretta, helps on Saturdays. Here, Masucci pauses in a conversation with customer Joe Potts.

Photographer:
David Brandt

''People's Choice'' is the name of the award-winning barbecue sauce concocted by Bob and Al Lawson. The brothers, who make their living manufacturing machine parts, planned to market their sauce after FDA approval. Describing the sauce as ''mild, with a little aftertaste,'' they listed its major ingredients: ketchup, tomato sauce, pepper, garlic and mustard.

Photographer:
John Kurtz

Reluctantly shaking sleep from their eyes in the light of early morning, Blake and Van Alexander of Overland Park face a new day. Blake, age 4, attends the Overland Park Christian Church pre-school while Van, 3, rotates to a different neighbor's house each morning. He is one of the participants in the neighborhood co-op baby-sitting brigade with which his mother, Dana, helps while Dad is at work.

Photographer:
Julie Robertson

Sponsor: WESTERN AUTO

Rome wasn't built in a day, and neither was this pipe organ located in the conference chamber of the Reorganized Church of Jesus Christ of Latter Day Saints (RLDS) auditorium in Independence, Mo. With 6,000 pipes, it took six months to assemble in 1959 and is one of the largest free-standing pipe organs in the United States. There are 18 organists on staff. The World Headquarters of the RLDS church seats 6,000 people.

Photographer:
Richard Schefter

The columns of the Nelson-Atkins Museum of Art cast an imposing shadow in this evening exterior view of the massive beaux arts structure. The museum was constructed with money from an endowment by *Kansas City Star* founder William Rockhill Nelson and funds from the estate of school teacher and philanthropist Mary Atkins. Opened in 1933, the Nelson houses one of the western world's most impressive collections of Oriental art. The museum would soon launch its first major traveling exhibition, a collection of works by Kansas City artist Thomas Hart Benton.

Photographer:
Michael Bailey

At the Southern Pacific yard in Kansas City, Kan., trains are fueled and attached to one another to provide the necessary power to pull the outbound load. This scene is repeated many times daily in railroad yards throughout the nation's second-busiest rail hub.

Photographer:
Bob Barrett

Fred Walker minds the store for one of his fellow tenants at the Westport Flea Market. Walker, one of the original tenants at the neighborhood bazaar, travels to Europe and the Orient to buy the paintings, art objects and bronzes he sells to his customers. The building housed the Kitty Clover Potato Chip factory before reopening as the Westport Flea Market in 1970.

Photographer:
Darrell Sampson

Security officer Monroe Beard works the night shift from 11 p.m. to 7 a.m. at Menorah Medical Center. Except for the landing of a Life Flight helicopter, all was quiet in the early morning hours of October 5.

Photographer:
Randy Braun

Scott McCormick, creative director at Valentine-Radford advertising agency, stands amid the collection of eclectic clutter from which he draws inspiration for such clients as Hallmark Cards, Pizza Hut, Butler Manufacturing and US Sprint. Founded in 1947, Valentine-Radford is the city's second largest advertising agency.

Photographer:
Rudy Yanez

Johnson County publisher Tom Leathers prepares for an editorial meeting to discuss *The Squire's* annual "Best of Kansas City" awards. Leathers, a Kansas City native, is a familiar face in local publishing circles and winner of many awards in journalism. His weekly publications are celebrating their 30th anniversary. Leathers also contributes daily commentary to a Kansas City radio station and for a dozen years has hosted his own nightly talk show on cable television.

Photographer:
Dale Wilcox

The rosy glow of daybreak is reflected in the towers of the Locarno apartment building on the Country Club Plaza. The vintage 1928 Plaza structure reopened in the spring of 1988 following a two-year renovation that fully restored the building's 110 units.

Photographer:
Don Wolf

An addiction to the sport led Robert Olinger, 26, (with lantern) and Frank Holloway, 29, on a midnight channel cat fishing spree. The Independence, Mo. residents are regulars at Lake Jacomo, catching fish to take with them on their winter hunting trips. Olinger is the owner of a dry cleaning store, and Holloway is a hairdresser. A dream of Olinger's is to someday become a professional bass fisherman.

Photographer:
Jim Rollo

Sponsor: BLUE CROSS AND BLUE SHIELD OF KANSAS CITY

At their One Kansas City Place office, Shook, Hardy & Bacon partners (clockwise from left) Steve Aliber, Jim Ash, Bob Kirkland and Kip Wiggins discuss pending litigation. Shook, Hardy & Bacon, the city's second largest law firm, is a general corporate firm specializing in products liability litigation, mergers and acquisitions, banking, labor and employment law. The firm employs 530 people in its Missouri and Kansas offices.

Photographer:
Tim Davis

Farris Racy drives a forklift at Batliner Paper, the city's only independently owned paper recycler. At Batliner's riverfront warehouse, used paper is sorted, shredded and bailed before being recycled and sold for use as everything from computer paper to baby diapers. Racy flashes the ''fresh'' sign, which he said means ''everything is where it's at.''

Photographer:
John Kurtz

Vaughn Cowden, a member of the Kansas City-based band Caribe, gets in some accordian practice on the banks of Brush Creek just south of the Plaza. Caribe plays reggae, ska and other Caribbean-influenced music at clubs throughout the Midwest.

Photographer:
Dale Monaghen

Near the Lake Jacomo marina in Fleming Park, Rich Ambrusko and his son take time to get acquainted with some web-footed friends on a crisp autumn afternoon. The white domestic mallards live at the park year-round, surviving on hand-outs from park visitors.

Photographer:
Charles Brenneke

Sponsor: CATHERINE RICKBONE

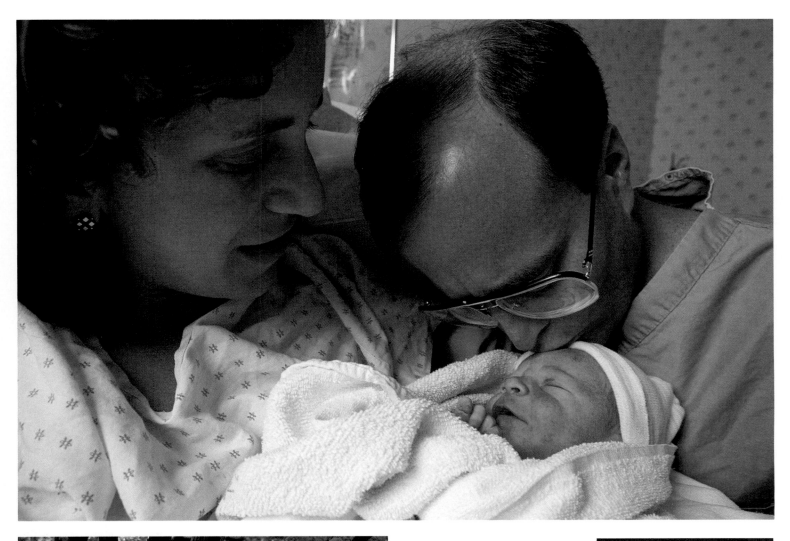

Daniel Aaron Flappan was among the youngest residents of Kansas City when this photo was taken at 12:30 a.m. October 5. Daniel, the son of Susan and Bob Flappan of Overland Park, weighed seven pounds, ¾ ounces when he was born at Menorah Medical Center at 10:42 p.m. October 4. Daniel joins five-year-old Michael in the Flappan household. "We had been trying for two years to have another baby, so it was a very special moment," says Susan. Daniel is "a very good and happy baby," according to his mother.

Photographer:
Randy Braun

Brad Richmond and his three-year-old son Tyler enjoy a mild autumn afternoon near their Overland Park home. Richmond's job as a cameraman at KCTV-5 requires him to work weekends, so he spends as much time as he can with Tyler on his midweek day off.

Photographer:
William Kirk

Clay Martin of Kansas City, Mo., is waiting for friends to join him after work at Kiki's Bon-Ton Maison restaurant in Westport. Martin, a self-employed tax and financial consultant, is a friend of the Cajun and Creole restaurant owners, Kiki and Richard Lucente. The restaurant is popular for its hot sauces which come from all over the world. Anyone bringing in a bottle of hot sauce receives a free drink, in keeping with the restaurant motto, "Laissez les bon temps rouler," French for "Let the good times roll."

Photographer:
Walt Whitaker

"Controlled violence" is the best way to describe the action on the trading floor as the opening bell sounded at the Kansas City Board of Trade. The world's largest marketplace for hard red winter wheat (which is used in bread), the Board of Trade has been in operation since 1876. On October 5, wheat for December, 1988, delivery closed at $4.17¼ cents per bushel, up 6¼ cents from the previous day.

Photographer:
Don Wolf

Wes Grimm (right) is a third generation tattoo artist, following in the footsteps of his grandfather, who established Grimm's Tattoo Parlour in 1913. Wes works on a design that incorporates a woman holding a Viking sword with a snake wrapped around her leg. The man's female companion waits patiently during the tattoo procedure.

Photographer:
Don Wolf

Seventeen-year-old Doug Shultz engages in the time-honored teen pastime of tying up the family phone. Perhaps the discussion is on his forthcoming graduation from Shawnee Mission Northwest High School, or his plans to attend the University of Kansas to study writing and filmmaking. His idol? Movie director Steven Spielberg, according to his mom, Laura, who took this shot.

Photographer:
Laura Maxwell Shultz

Kansas City Chiefs team members Kevin Porter (left) and Neil Smith have the look of winners off the field, even though the Chiefs posted only a 4-11-1 record during the 1988 season. Porter, the team's safety, was a third-round draft pick in 1988 from Auburn University. He started in seven games, garnering 64 tackles. Defensive end Smith, the Chiefs' 1988 first-round draft choice from Nebraska College, started in seven games and made 53 tackles and 2.5 sacks. Porter and Smith will be playing for new head coach Marty Schottenheimer during the 1989 season. Schottenheimer replaced Frank Ganz, who was fired after failing to lead the Chiefs to a winning season.

Photographer:
John Kurtz

Stan Whitmore (standing), area manager of the Christian Broadcasting Network's 700 Club, leads his staff in a daily prayer meeting. Kansas City is one of 40 ministry centers serving the nationally broadcast televangelist network. With a local staff of seven and about 350 volunteers, 700 Club members maintain a 24-hour prayer line, sometimes fielding up to 1,000 calls in a 24-hour period when the network's 800-line is routed through the group's Shawnee office.

Photographer:
Wally Emerson

Officer Dan Taylor of the Central Patrol Division frisks a suspect outside Sanderson's Lunch at 38th & Main. The man allegedly left the restaurant without paying his check and walked into the waiting arms of the law as Taylor patrolled his beat. The situation was resolved, and no arrest was made. Taylor, a Kansas City native, is a one-year veteran with the Police Department. He is assigned to Watch One from 10 p.m. to 6 a.m.

Photographer:
Chris Cannella

Taking a break a the pool table is Tom Cullen, general manager of Westport's Guitars & Cadillacs, a country and western night club that opened in June, 1988. Cullen has done everything from shoveling during construction to hiring employees and ordering supplies. The popular night spot was named for a record album featuring country artist Dwight Yoakum. As many as 1,500 guests are entertained at Guitars & Cadillacs during a typical weekend, says Cullen.

Photographer:
Walt Whitaker

Clemia Bennett, a customer at the midtown Silo store, pauses to observe the action during the vice-presidential debate held on October 5. Bennett, a Democrat, said he planned to vote the Dukakis-Bentsen ticket . . . which went down to defeat.

Photographer:
Charles Kneyse

Ellington Bell, assistant drill master with the Marching Cobras, rehearses a high-stepping routine with the popular drill team. Originally an all-male team established by instructor Willie Smith at Lincoln High School in 1970, the group has expanded to include 112 members — both boys and girls — from all over the city. The Cobras have performed at the White House for President Reagan and at the Cotton Bowl in 1980, 1981 and 1982. Their appearances have taken them to 43 different states and to Europe.

Photographer:
Suzanne Robinson

State Ballet of Missouri company members (left to right) Brian Staihr, Jody Atkinson and Klas Campbell limber up at the ballet's Westport rehearsal studio. The company was preparing for its fall performance, which included ''Les Sylphides,'' Alvin Ailey's ''The River'' and ''Enough Said,'' a new ballet by Kansas-born Clark Tippet of the American Ballet Theatre. In his October 14 review of the program, *Kansas City Star* music editor Kenneth LaFave singled out Atkinson and Staihr for their ''smolderingly sexual duet'' on ''The River.''

Photographer:
Victor Almo

Mike Riley, a sophomore at
Shawnee Mission Northwest High
School, mimics the action on a
mural in downtown Kansas City.
The mural was painted as part of
the city's preparations for the
Final Four basketball tournament
in the spring of 1988.

Photographer:
Randy Braun

Shawnee Mission South High
School senior Heather Poncez
prepares to put one over the net
during a practice game in the
school gymnasium. The Raiders
volleyball team won about 70
percent of its games, entitling the
team to a spot on the state tournament roster. Poncez, a two-year
letter winner in volleyball,
qualified for a full volleyball
scholarship to a Florida college.

Photographer:
Mike Mihalevich

A pickup basketball game at the City Hall court in Overland Park, Kan., glows with an eerie light. Photographer John Kurtz positioned himself near the floor of the court and used a flash to illuminate the players in this twilight contest.

Photographer:
John Kurtz

Sponsor: NORTH KANSAS CITY HOSPITAL

◁ Since 1975, Richard Renner, 31, has worked as an actor, juggler, and stilt-walking character. On national Hyatt "Vote America Day" at the Hyatt Regency Crown Center Hotel, Renner dressed as a tall Uncle Sam to encourage absentee balloting for travelers and general public voter registration. Here Renner greets a voter of the future.

Photographer:
Walt Whitaker

◁ With an assist from mother Gina Frazee, two-year-old Jenifer Frazee gets a closer look at an inquisitive giraffe in the African veldt section at the Kansas City Zoo. The giraffe is one of two on display at the zoo, which is the city's third most popular tourist attraction.

Photographer:
Jeff Altwies

Kansas City International Airport is home to 16 air carriers, including three regional commuter lines. Opened in 1972 at a cost of $250 million, KCI is the nation's second youngest airport. More than nine million passengers pass through its gates every year.

Photographer:
Chris Cannella

Air traffic control specialist Matt Ross (left) monitors the "separation," or distance between arriving and departing aircraft, in the tower at Kansas City International Airport, while supervisor Carey Rolofson looks on. On October 5, KCI recorded 1,026 arrivals and departures, a typical number on an average day at the Nation's 30th largest airport.

Photographer:
Chris Cannella

Sponsor: AAA AUTO CLUB

(left to right) Tiberius Klausner, Paul J. Hatton, Robert Battey and Hugh Brown, members of the Volker String Quartet, conduct a rehearsal at the University of Missouri-Kansas City's Conservatory of Music. Klausner is concertmaster with the Kansas City Symphony, in which violinists Hatton and Brown perform as well. All four members of the resident ensemble serve on the conservatory faculty. The group has performed at the Kennedy Center in Washington and in concerts throughout the Midwest.

Photographer:
Terry Weckbaugh

Sean Gibbs, 17, a senior at Shawnee Mission West High School, hopes to pursue a career as a professional musician. A guitarist with the punk band Raw (War spelled backwards), Sean has been playing professionally since he was 15. He plans to study music at William Jewell College.

Photographer:
Dan Dakotas

Musician Eddie Baker rehearses
the Kansas City Jazz Orchestra as
they prepare for a performance at
the October 9 Kansas City
premiere of ''Bird,'' a film
biography of jazz great Charlie
Parker. The 17-piece jazz
ensemble represents the Charlie
Parker Memorial Foundation,
where youngsters receive musical
instruction from seasoned Kansas
City jazz veterans. Parker was a
native Kansas Citian.

Photographer:
Ray Corey

Sponsor: ROCKHURST COLLEGE

After Independence, Mo., fireman
Captain John Holman was the
target of a sniper's gunshots on
October 4, KCTV-5 reporter Marty
Lanus interviewed Independence
assistant fire chief Ben Jones for a
next-day follow-up news story.
The fireman was treated for minor
injuries. Lanus, an 18-year veteran
reporter, has been with KCTV-5
since 1979.

Photographer:
Brenda Grazda

Returning home after completing his "Focus Kansas City" assignments, photographer Don Wolf was among the first on the scene of this truck fire on Interstate 635 near State Avenue in Kansas City, Kan. To capture the moment on film, Wolf negotiated his way through oncoming traffic and steadied his camera on the guard rail separating the north and southbound lanes.

Photographer:
Don Wolf

Little metroplex on the prairie: an ▷ area that was once a flat field is adorned with yet another office building. The towering silhouettes of a construction site at sunrise caught the eye of photographer John Blasdel. The building is a Properties of America office building located near 110th and Metcalf in Overland Park, Kan.

Photographer:
John Blasdel

The Missouri River's muddy waters ▷ turn to gold in an October sunset. The vantage point is the south bank of the river, just downstream from the Paseo Bridge.

Photographer:
Ron Berg

Father Tom Culhane celebrates
morning mass at St. Ann's Church
in Prairie Village, where he has
been the pastor for five years. The
congregation of about 1500
families was preparing to celebrate
its 40th anniversary in 1989.

Photographer:
Wally Emerson

Missouri Repertory Theater founder Dr. Patricia McIlrath is captured in a reflective mood at her Plaza area apartment. Dr. McIlrath founded MRT in 1964 and served as its artistic director until her retirement in 1985. She maintains her lifelong interest in the theater, and is busy compiling a history of MRT.

Photographer:
Kerry Kohrs

Jerry Talifero, who at 6'5'' has earned the nickname ''Stick,'' is one of the periodic residents of the City Union Mission. The institution in the City Market area averages 55 to 60 overnight residents daily. Union officials say that number climbs even higher in cold weather.

Photographer:
Lauren Chapin

The Barney Allis Plaza fountain is a high-tech addition to the City of Fountains. Designed by the same firm responsible for the water displays at Disney's Epcot Center, the $1.2 million fountain holds 50,000 gallons of water, with 112 geysers and 288 multi-colored lights. Both the water and light displays are controlled by a computer program. The fountain was dedicated September 11, 1985.

Photographer:
Darrell Sampson

The sun's warming rays break through the silhouetted skyline of downtown Kansas City as dawn breaks October 5.

Photographer:
Chris Cannella

Sponsor: COMMERCE BANK

Because Kansas City is the largest hub of Braniff, the company shoots many of its television commercials here. This view of a jetliner lifting off was shot even as a video crew was photographing the same scene. Braniff, which now employs more than 1,500 workers here, accounts for more flights than any other airline.

Photographer:
John Vawter

Once a mechanic, always a mechanic. Dutch Huston, 61, is a retired TWA mechanic from Liberty, Mo., and one of many retirees who helped restore this Lockheed Constellation at the downtown Municipal Airport. The project, dubbed ''Save A Connie,'' began in 1985 with volunteers rebuilding the 1959-vintage aircraft that saw duty in Vietnam as a cargo plane. The group plans to take the craft to airshows and other exhibitions.

Photographer:
Chuck Roderique

Major George D. Burgess is assistant operations officer of the 303rd Tactical Fighter Squadron, attached to the 442nd Tactical Fighter Wing at Richards Gebaur Air Force Base. Burgess, whose call sign is ''Farmer,'' lives on a farm near Harrisonville, Mo. As an air reserve technician, Burgess is a full-time civil service employee who also maintains active status in the Air Force Reserve. He flies an A-10 Thunderbolt II aircraft, also known as the ''tank killer,'' which is designed to provide air support for ground maneuvers.

Photographer:
Mike Mihalevich

Tim Mershon is the fourth-generation farmer to work his family's 1,000-acre spread in Buckner, Mo. Although many farms suffered ill effects from the drought of 1988, the Mershons reported that their crops survived the lack of rainfall.

Photographer:
Ben Weddle

As evening shadows grow deeper, Tom Mershon finishes a 12-hour day of harvesting corn on the family's farm in Buckner, Mo.

Photographer:
Ben Weddle

A group of Greenpeace protesters assembled outside the Environmental Protection Agency in downtown Kansas City, Kan., to call attention to environmental issues such as noise reduction, industrial waste and air and water pollution. The protesters were vocal, but peaceful, and nobody complained about the noise level.

Photographer:
Vernon Leat

111

Corky Weston is called "the world's greatest welder" by his co-workers, but Corky himself expresses a modest satisfaction with his work. An iron worker and welder for 36 years, Corky says the rewards of his job are "being able to look back and see what you've done." This particular project was welding structural steel for the food court section of One Kansas City Place, a 42-story office tower in downtown Kansas City.

Photographer:
Bob Barrett

Restaurant owner Ruby McIntyre dishes up conversation along with a unique menu in Kansas City — chitlins, pig hocks with black-eyed peas, collard greens and more — at Ruby's Soul Food Cafe. McIntyre began cooking at the age of three on a plantation in Tennessee. She was a cook for William Jewell College before opening her own restaurant at 15th and Brooklyn in 1952. McIntyre tried to retire in 1985, but it lasted only three months; her displaced customers took to stopping by her house for breakfast. When 20 hungry people showed up at her doorstep one morning, Ruby decided it was time to go back to work.

Photographer:
William Kirk

Retirement is a dirty word to 85-year-old Hans Rudolph, founder and chairman of the board of Hans Rudolph, Inc., a respiratory valve manufacturing company. Rudolph, whose son and grandson are president and vice president, respectively, of the company, is a German immigrant who came to America at the age of 21. He began designing medical devices at Indiana University, and since 1940 has had his own business distributing his wares. He is shown holding a breathing valve used for respiratory testing in hospitals.

Photographer:
Gilbert Snedden

When the American Hereford Association built its headquarters at 715 Hereford Drive, its landmark bull statue stirred a controversy. "No one wanted the bull's rear end to face their direction," said Dewey Rounds of the American Hereford Association. But someone lost; the bull faces north. Made of steel and plastic, the bull weighs three tons. The original headquarters was dedicated by President Dwight Eisenhower in 1953, but the association has since relocated to a newer building at 1501 Wyandotte.

Photographer:
Darrell Sampson

At Acme Neon in the River Market, Ron Ogborn completes a neon fixture that will be installed in the Mrs. Fields Cookies shop in Ward Parkway. Ogborn is at the "blocking out" stage, applying a special paint to the glass so that connecting lines will be less noticeable. Ogborn says the neon sign business is booming since its rebirth on the west coast. By combining the argon or blue gases and neon or red gases with different colors of glass, Acme produces nearly 100 shades for its clients.

Photographer:
Suzanne Robinson

Artist Philomene Bennett works on a commissioned portrait in her home studio. Bennett's historic Lenexa farmhouse was scheduled for demolition as part of a road improvement project. She subsequently moved to Santa Fe, New Mexico, but maintains a studio in Kansas City.

Photographer:
Dan Dakotas

Louie Dunham practices his trade as a horseshoer at the Sutherland Farm, 121st and Nall in Overland Park. Dunham has been shoeing horses since he was graduated from high school in 1970, pursuing an interest nurtured by his father.

Photographer:
Dan Dakotas

Kansas City Star columnist C.W. Gusewelle, a *Star* staffer for more than 30 years, entertains readers with his sometimes whimsical, often thought-provoking insights into the human condition. In addition to his newspaper columns, Gusewelle's short stories and essays have appeared in *Harper's, American Heritage* and other magazines. He was the recipient of *Paris Review's* Aga Kahn Prize for Fiction in 1977.

Photographer:
Jeff Vaughn

Thang Tu Pham, an employee of the XSIS Electronics Inc. in Shawnee, Kan., inspects a clock oscillator digital timing device that will become part of a military weapons system computer. XSIS supplies parts to military contractors worldwide.

Photographer:
John Mutrux

Black belt karate instructor Erick McEnaney demonstrates all the right moves at the American Kenpo Karate Academy. McEnaney began his training in 1979, and competed in the National Finals Karate Championship in Oklahoma City in 1982 and 1985. The 26-year-old Kansas City native practices Chinese boxing, which combines traditional martial arts maneuvers with boxing.

Photographer:
Randy Braun

Tatiana Dokoudovska, known to generations of ballet students as "Miss Tania," focuses a watchful eye on dance students at the University of Missouri-Kansas City Conservatory of Music. Dokoudovska came to Kansas City from New York to join the resident ballet company at Starlight Theater in 1954. A direct descendent of the Russian czar Ivan the Terrible, Dokoudovska was born in Monte Carlo and danced with the Ballets Russes and the Ballet Theater, which later became the American Ballet Theater. She helped build the dance department at the Conservatory, where she has been an instructor for more than 30 years.

Photographer:
Terry Weckbaugh

Sponsor: UNIVERSITY OF MISSOURI-KANSAS CITY SCHOOL OF DENTISTRY

he left to become an independent book producer and consultant.

President of the National Press Photographers Association in 1975 and 1976, he was twice chairman of the Pictures of the Year competition sponsored jointly by NPPA and the University of Missouri. He helped found the National Press Photographers Foundation and is a trustee of the William Allen White Foundation of the University of Kansas. Clarkson is currently a member of the editorial committee of the American Society of Magazine Photographers.

Clarkson is a regular lecturer at the annual Missouri Workshops, the Maine Photographic Workshops, the International Center of Photography in New York and the American Press Institute. He was a lecturer at the University of Kansas School of Journalism for seven years and a Pulitzer Prize juror in 1985-86.

The award-winning photographer is a contributor to numerous publications on photojournalism and sports and has co-authored five books: "The Jim Ryun Story" with Cordner Nelson in 1967, "Sooner" with Bill Bruns in 1972, "Knight With the Hoosiers" with Bill Hammel in 1975, "Montreal '76" with Bill Bruns in 1976 and "The Final Four" with Billy Reed in 1988. He was producer-coordinator for a Brian Lanker project, "I Dream A World, Portraits of Black Women Who Changed America" published as a book and traveling exhibition in 1989. Director of Photography for the book, "A Day in the Life of America" in 1986, Clarkson was also a photographer on four "Day in the Life" projects.

Active as a magazine photographer, he currently is under contract to *Sports Illustrated* as one of its contributing photographers. His work has appeared regularly over the years in *Time*, *Life* and *The Saturday Evening Post*. Clarkson has photographed six summer and one winter Olympics. He organized the picture coverage for *Time* at Munich in 1972 and Montreal in 1976, and for *Sports Illustrated* in Moscow in 1980. He was also a consultant to the Los Angeles Organizing Committee for the 1984 summer games.

Now based in Denver, Clarkson is an independent producer/editor of photographic books, exhibits and workshops.

Rick Cusick
Book Designer

Rick Cusick is admired as one of this country's outstanding book designers. For 11 of his 18 years at Hallmark Cards, Cusick designed books for the company — which he now serves as a master artist in the Lettering and Typography Department. He passes on his expertise to University of Kansas students who take his course there in editorial and publication design.

Since 1974, Cusick has been associated with TBW Books in Woolwich, Maine, as a design and editorial consultant. In 1979, he was elected into the Bund Deutscher Buchkünstler (Association of German Book Artists). At this time he also initiated Nyx Editions, a non-commercial publishing venture for his personal publications.

Besides his design of the beautiful *Fountains of Kansas City*, Cusick's book design credits include *With Respect . . . to RFD*, a book about the life and work of Chicago designer and calligrapher Raymond Franklin DaBoll; *Straight Impressions*, a collection of articles and examples of calligraphy by Lloyd J. Reynolds; and *The Proverbial Bestiary*, a collection of proverbs from around the world that was a Book of the Month Club selection.

Born in 1947 in Stockton, Calif., Cusick pursued an interest in design and calligraphy at San Joaquin Delta College in Stockton. After graduation, he worked at Ad/Art, Inc., designing illuminated signs. He also attended Art Center College of Design in Los Angeles.

Professional affiliations include ATypI (Association Typographique Internationale), Typocrafters and the New York Type Directors Club.

Cusick is currently at work assembling an exhibition focusing on his work in the book arts. His 1987 one-man exhibition of lettering and typography appeared at the Appleman Gallery in London.

Cusick's work has appeared in numerous books and periodicals, including *Typography 6, International Calligraphy Today, Communication Arts* and *Fine Print*.

His work also has been included in numerous exhibitions throughout the world, the latest being

Rick Cusick, recognized internationally for his work in book design and calligraphy, was responsible for the organization and placement of the photographs in Focus Kansas City.

"AKARA, An Exhibition on World Calligraphy," a traveling exhibition that was launched at the Indira Ghandi National Centre for the Arts in New Delhi.

He also participated in the 1989 International Book Design exhibition, "Peace and the Book," in Leipzig, East Germany.

Steve Wilson
Screening Committee

Steve Wilson obtained a bachelor's degree in photography and printmaking from East Texas State University in 1982. He worked as a professional musician and at portrait and commercial photography studios in Texas and Oklahoma before joining Hallmark Cards as a senior photographer in 1985. Wilson works for the greeting card design and specialty products divisions at Hallmark, producing photographs for the company's greeting cards, calendars and puzzles. Married and the father of three children, Wilson enjoys woodworking and photography in his spare time.

Larry Nicholson
Screening Committee

A graduate of William Jewell College, Larry Nicholson began his career as a photographer/writer/producer/director in 1954. His company, Nicholson Communications, has now completed over 9,000 projects and assignments for clients nationwide. His photographs have appeared in such publications as *Time, Newsweek, National Geographic* and *Farm Journal*. Nicholson's advertising and illustration photography has appeared in many publications and on television. Since 1971, Nicholson has produced an annual multi-image show for World Championship Tennis in Dallas, in conjunction with the finals of the World Series of Tennis. For five years, he served as writer and technical director for "Families Are Forever," an elaborate outdoor pageant held in Independence, Mo. Nicholson's work has received numerous awards from Eastman Kodak, the New York Film Festival, the Kansas City Art Directors Club and others.

Rob Eisele and Jody Buie acted as coordinators, researchers and writers for much of the text in Focus Kansas City.

Robert Eisele
Editorial Associate

Robert Eisele, a native of Kansas City, graduated from the University of Missouri-Kansas City.

A former member of the *Kansas City Star* staff, Eisele's work has appeared in such publications as *USA Today, Midwest Living* and *Guest Informant*.

Eisele served as *Kansas City* magazine's drama critic, and his movie reviews have appeared in American City Business Journal publications nationwide. Eisele's reviews of books, theater and music appear regularly in the *Kansas City Star*. He was a 1982 critic fellow at the Eugene O'Neill Theater Center in Waterford, Conn.

As an editorial associate for Harrow Books, Eisele coordinated much of the preparation of cutlines and additional copy for *Focus Kansas City*.

While serving as information specialist for the Prime Time News Bureau, Eisele helped develop strategies for a national media relations program on behalf of the Kansas City Area Economic Development Council.

At Waddell & Reed, a national financial services organization headquartered in Kansas City, Eisele edited money management publications for the company's sales force of financial planning representatives.

Eisele also is a past vice-president and board member of the Kansas City chapter of the International Association of Business Communicators.

Jody Buie
Editorial Assistant

Jody Buie, editorial assistant for Harrow Books, is a 1976 graduate of Shawnee Mission North High School, where she was feature editor of the school newspaper. Buie received an associate's degree from Calvary Bible College in 1983. She edited the school's newspaper, then remained with the college to work as an assistant to the director of public ministries. She developed a quarterly newsletter for prospective students and was editorial assistant for the *Calvary Review* magazine. Since 1985, Buie has been the host of a 15-minute radio program, "Consumer Comment," heard weekly over KLJC FM, the radio station of Calvary Bible College.

Buie's writing has appeared in such magazines as *Seventeen, Reader's Digest* and *Conquest*. Most recently, she helped develop "Singleminded," a quarterly newsletter for single women, and serves as its editor and designer.

Buie assisted with interviewing, gathering information and writing cutlines for many of the "Focus Kansas City" photographs. She currently is working on her bachelor of arts degree in communications from Ottawa University.

Production Art

A special word of appreciation for the sharp eyes and steady hands of artists Connie Robinson, Steve Mulanax and Bense Garza, who were responsible for the physical assembly of type, art and photographs in preparation for printing.

Thank you.

In any project of this magnitude, dozens of friends and associates lend helpful support of one sort or another. Sometimes it is a creative suggestion; sometimes just a word of advice or encouragement. The following persons, listed in a random order, did just that. Inevitably, I will have forgotten someone by name, but not their kindness. –D.S.H.

Edna Frederikson, William F. Caldwell, Herbert Adler, Ginzy Schaefer, Steve Doyal, Judy Hutson, Michael Mihalevich, Bob Barrett, David Wirtz, Debbie Burch, Shifra Stein, Catherine Rickbone, Gerard Eisterhold, Cynthia Siebert, John Elliott, Tom Rafferty, Don Forsythe, Walt Bodine, Janet Reading, Hannah Cusick, Ralph Waterhouse, Linda Best, Katherine Huseby, Roger McDougle, Charles Mallory, Mia Katz, Jackie Hudson, Jim Arnold, Pat Dunsmore, Mary Adams, Dinah Hudson, Roy Inman, David Hutson, Ralph Rowe, Jo Bennett, Jill Adams, Coral Moulder, Linda Friedel, Jeffie Mussman, Tony Hallaba, Tracy Nohe, Jim Hale, Linda Friedel, Bill Gilgus, Dennie Cody, Eileen Wirtz, Tom Bodine, Steve Bell, Dana Eisele, Richie Cusick, David Westbrook, Pam McCarthy, Betty Lynn Gregg.